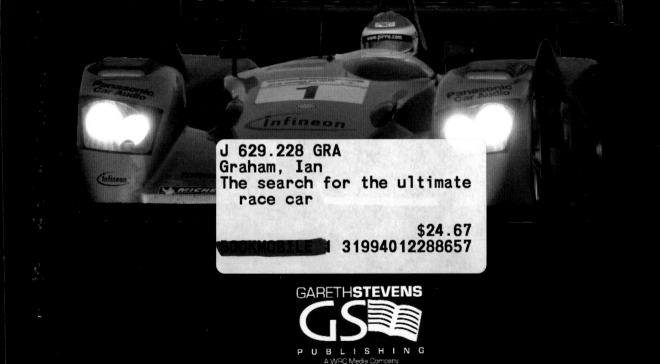

GARETH**STEVENS**
GS
P U B L I S H I N G
A WRC Media Company

Please visit our web site at: www.garethstevens.com
For a free color catalog describing Gareth Stevens Publishing's list of high-quality books
and multimedia programs, call 1-800-542-2595 (USA) or 1-800-387-3178 (Canada).
Gareth Stevens Publishing's fax: (414) 332-3567.

Library of Congress Cataloging-in-Publication Data

Graham, Ian.
    The search for the ultimate race car / by Ian Graham. — North American ed.
        p. cm. — (Science quest)
    Includes index.
    ISBN 0-8368-4558-7 (lib. bdg.)
    1. Automobiles, Racing—Design and construction—Juvenile literature.
  I. Title. II. Series.
  TL236.G694   2005
  629.228—dc22   2004059002

This North American edition first published in 2005 by
Gareth Stevens Publishing
A World Almanac® Education Group Company
330 West Olive Street, Suite 100
Milwaukee, WI 53212 USA

This U.S. edition copyright © 2005 by Gareth Stevens, Inc. Original edition copyright © 2004 by ticktock Entertainment Ltd.
First published in Great Britain in 2004 by ticktock Media Ltd., Unit 2, Orchard Business Centre, North Farm Road,
Tunbridge Wells, Kent, TN2 3XF.

Gareth Stevens editor: Jim Mezzanotte
Gareth Stevens designer: Kami M. Koenig
Consultant: Bryan Yagar

Photo Credits: (t=top, b=bottom, c=center, l=left, r=right)
Action Plus: 2-3 (all), 4-5 (all), 7(r), 8 (t), 12(t), 14 (all), 15 (all), 18 (all), 19 (all), 22, 29 (bl), 29(t). Alamy: 12 (b), 28,
29 (br). Car Photo Library: 6 (bl). Motoring Picture Library: 6-7 (c), 10-11 (t). Redzone: 10 (b), 20 (t), 23 (b), 26-27 (t), 27
(b). Science Photo Library: 13, 20 (b). Sporting Images: 6 (tl), 8 (b), 10 (tl), 11 (b), 16 (c), 17, 21 (all), 23(t), 24-25 (c), 25
(b), 26 (b).

Printed in the United States of America

1 2 3 4 5 6 7 8 9 09 08 07 06 05

Contents

Car racing makes use of the most advanced science, **technology**, materials, and **engineering** to build the fastest cars. When the first race between cars was held in France in 1894, the winning car had an average speed of 10.19 miles (16.4 kilometers) per hour. Since then, race car teams have searched for every possible way of making their cars go faster.

The Science of Speed

A team of people is involved in the science of creating a fast car. Some people design the shapes of race cars, using **aerodynamics**. **Chemists** create the fuels and oils used in race car engines. Other people are responsible for the advanced materials with which the cars are built. Computer scientists develop electronic systems that control the engines, and they create the computer systems that are used to design the cars. Race teams also use computers to test computer models of their cars. **Physicists** and mathematicians calculate the forces that act on cars during a race. Engineers bring the work of all these scientists together to build the cars.

Working Within the Rules

Race car designers are not able to use all the advances in materials, fuel, oil, computers, electronics, and aerodynamics that they would like, because they have to work within the rules of the sport. If the organizations that set the rules decide that the race cars are becoming too fast, they may change the rules to slow the cars down. If some teams are spending huge amounts of money on new technology that other teams cannot afford, the organizations may change the rules to ensure fair competition. Of all the various race car sports, **Formula One** racing gives car designers the most freedom to use advanced science and technology.

NASCAR race cars hug the track as they bank a turn at a speed of up to 186 miles (300 km) per hour.

Brazilian driver Cristiano Da Matta sits in a Toyota during a Formula One test session.

From Track to Street

Some of the advanced technology used in race cars is later applied to ordinary cars, to make them safer, more **efficient**, and more reliable. Today's cars use **innovations** in brakes, tires, engines, and materials that were first tested in race cars. The science of creating race cars is never finished, because race teams are constantly looking for new ways to make their cars go faster. New developments in science and technology make new advances in car design possible. Racing rules change frequently, so teams have to keep creating new cars.

*Gary Scelzi sits in the **cockpit** of his **dragster** at the 38th Annual Pontiac Excitement Nationals, held at National Trail Raceway in Hebron, Ohio.*

Race driver David Coulthard squeezes into the tiny cockpit of his race car.

Race cars go faster if they are the right shape. Some shapes slip through the air more easily than others. The study of what happens to objects when they move through air is called aerodynamics. Race car designers use aerodynamics to create the fastest body shapes.

Slim Bodies

Race cars have smooth, gently curving bodies to help them slip through the air. The body of a single-seat race car is very slim for the same reason. A driver has just enough room to wriggle down inside, but only if the steering wheel has been removed! Single-seat race cars are also very low. Drivers have to lie on their backs when they drive.

SCIENCE CONCEPTS

Reducing Drag

When a car moves, it has to push air out of its way. The air pushes back. The effect of the air pushing back against the car is called air resistance, or **drag**. Some car shapes produce less drag than others. A race car or sports car, such as this Ferrari F50, is designed to create very little drag. It has a **streamlined** body shape. The air streams easily around the car when it is moving.

Wings at Work

Race cars have wings so they can go around turns faster. When a race car takes a turn at a high speed, it might skid off the track. Advanced **suspension** and wide tires help keep it on the track. Wings are also a big help. They create **downforce**.

> *Wings enable cars to go around turns at high speeds, without skidding off the track.*

This force pushes down on the car's wheels, so the tires grip the track better.

A race car has wings in the front and in the back. They are like upside-down airplane wings. The wings of an airplane lift it into the air. A race car's wings create the opposite effect, pushing down on the car. The downforce created by these wings is extremely powerful. With these wings, a race car traveling at 100 miles (160 km) per hour could drive upside-down along the roof of a tunnel without falling off!

Airfoil Effect

Like an airplane wing, a race car wing is an **airfoil**. It creates a certain force when air flows past it. A race car's wing has the opposite shape of an airplane wing. It is flatter on the top and more curved on the bottom. When the car is moving, air flowing beneath the wing has to travel farther across the wing's curve than air flowing over the wing's top. The pressure of the air is less beneath the wing, creating suction that pulls the car downward.

SCIENCE SNAPSHOT

Designers test the shapes of race cars in wind tunnels. A wind tunnel is an enclosed area with air blowing through it. Race car designers began using wind tunnels in the 1960s. Today, aerodynamics is so important that some car racing teams have their own wind tunnels. Some wind tunnels test scale models of cars. Others are big enough to test full-size cars.

Ready to be tested, a scale model of a Formula One car sits in a wind tunnel.

An engine makes a car move by burning **fuel**. When the fuel burns, its energy is released. The energy causes the engine's **crankshaft** to spin. This spinning motion turns the car's wheels. A race car's engine is designed to convert the heat of burning fuel into movement as quickly as possible.

This Formula One race car engine was used in the 1999 season. It has ten cylinders, arranged in the shape of a "V," with five cylinders on each side. This kind of engine is called a V10 engine.

Firepower

Engines work by burning fuel inside metal tubes called **cylinders**. Formula One race car engines must have ten cylinders. Other race cars often have eight-cylinder engines. Air is sucked into each cylinder and fuel is added. Then, a tight-fitting **piston** slides up the cylinder and squashes the mixture of fuel and air. An electric spark causes the fuel to burn, heating the air in the cylinder. The heat makes the air expand. The expanding air pushes the piston back down the cylinder with great force. Each piston is attached to the crankshaft. The up-and-down movements, or **strokes**, of all the pistons turns the crankshaft, providing the power to turn the car's wheels. Engine power is measured in **horsepower**. A race car engine can produce a huge amount of horsepower.

SCIENCE CONCEPTS

Internal Combustion

Car engines are internal **combustion** engines. Combustion, or burning, is a chemical reaction between fuel and air that gives off heat. To get the best performance from a race car's engine, air has to mix with the fuel so the fuel burns quickly. Engineers design the best shape for the tops of cylinders so fuel and air mix well inside them.

SCIENCE SNAPSHOT

Fuel only burns when it is mixed with air. Engines burn more fuel if extra air is forced into them. An engine that burns more fuel is more powerful, so the car will be faster. A machine called a **turbocharger** blows more air into an engine. Champ cars and some street cars, such as certain cars made by Porsche, have turbocharged engines.

This Porsche sports car is powered by a turbocharged engine.

Race Car Fuels

Different race cars burn different types of fuel. Formula One cars burn gasoline. Cars in the **Champ Car World Series** and the **Indy Racing League** burn a fuel called **methanol**. Methanol is a single chemical, but gasoline is a complicated mixture of several chemicals. Chemists can produce different mixtures, or blends, of gasoline to suit different engines and even different racetracks. Top Formula One race teams have their own fuel scientists who work to produce the right fuel for their cars.

Slippery Science

When an engine is running, oil flows through it, coating all the moving parts. The oil is a **lubricant** that makes the parts slippery, so they rub against each other without sticking. Oil is especially important to race car engines, because they work much faster than normal engines. Every time a race car is driven, team members test the oil. Tiny metal specks in the oil tell them how fast the engine's moving parts are wearing down and if anything is going wrong inside.

Tire Technology

The rubber for race car tires is made from more than one hundred ingredients.

A race car's tires are its only link to the ground. The tires have to handle the engine's immense power and keep the car on the track at very high speeds. Race car tires have to grip the ground without sliding. The tires also have to withstand forces that try to tear them apart during a race. They are very different from ordinary tires.

Big At the Back

In most race cars, the engine drives the rear wheels. The rear tires are taller and wider than the front tires, because they need to grip the road when the engine turns them. Bigger tires put more rubber to the ground and grip the road better, especially in turns. The front tires are smaller to help the car's aerodynamics. They cause less drag.

Racing Rubber

Race car tires are made of a special type of rubber. The tires are softer and stickier than normal tires. They grip the road better, but they wear out quicker. A normal tire lasts up to 60,000 miles (96,500 km). A Formula One tire lasts only about 125 miles (200 km)! During a race, drivers have to stop to have worn-out tires changed.

SCIENCE CONCEPTS

Tires and Friction

Friction, which enables a race car's tires to grip the ground, is a force that works to stop objects from sliding against each other. More friction occurs between surfaces when they are rough and dry. Less friction occurs when the surfaces are smooth and wet. Race cars are more likely to skid on a wet track, because water reduces the friction between the tires and the track.

Race cars are fitted with tires that are suited to the weather conditions during a race. A team has to choose the right tires in order to win.

Tires for the Weather

A **slick**, or tire with a smooth tread, puts the most rubber in contact with the ground. This kind of tire creates the most grip, but only on a dry track. If a track is wet, water gets between the tires and the track. The tires may then aquaplane, which means they ride on a thin film of water and do not actually come into contact with the ground. During rainy weather, racing teams use different tires. These tires have grooves that force water out from under them, for better contact with the ground. In Formula One racing, dry-weather tires also have grooves, to make the racing more difficult.

SCIENCE SNAPSHOT

As a car travels, its tires heat up. The rubber used in race car tires gives the most grip when it is hot. This rubber works best at a temperature of about 212° Fahrenheit (100° Celsius), which is hot enough to boil water! Before a race, Formula One teams wrap the race cars' wheels in electric blankets to heat the tires up to the right temperature, so they give a lot of grip right from the start. When a race car needs new tires during a race, the tires are heated before they are put on the car.

Tire warmers prepare a BMW Williams Formula One car for a practice session before the 2003 Monaco Grand Prix.

R ace cars are made from a variety of different materials. Some race cars are made from traditional materials, such as steel, but many race car builders use new, advanced materials. These materials are strong, but they are also very light. A light car **accelerates** faster than a heavier car.

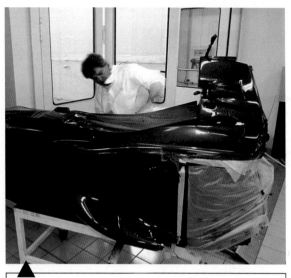

At first, a race car is black, which is the color of carbon fiber. Later, the car is painted with the team's colors.

Carbon Fiber

Race cars used to be made from steel and other metals. Today, however, most race cars are built with a material called **carbon fiber**. More than four-fifth of a Formula One race car is made from carbon fiber. It is used because it is one-quarter the weight of steel but twice as strong. Carbon fiber is made from long, threadlike fibers of carbon that are woven together to form mats. The mats are soaked in a liquid plastic called resin. At first, the resin stays in liquid form, so the mats can be molded into any shape. Then, the resin hardens, and the result is a strong but lightweight material. To ensure that the resin hardens in exactly the right way, the carbon fiber parts are baked at a carefully controlled temperature in a special oven. The carbon fiber is used to construct a race car's main frame, or **chassis**. The engine, suspension, and other parts are attached to the chassis. Carbon fiber is also used to make the car's nose and wings.

SCIENCE CONCEPTS

Plentiful Polymers

Carbon fiber is a type of material called a **polymer**. There are many polymers in nature. Diamonds, natural rubber, and some parts of plants are polymers. Our bodies contain substances called proteins, which are also polymers. Scientists can make polymers by adding  many simple chemical units, called monomers, together to form long chains (above). Polymers made in laboratories include nylon, polythene, polystyrene, and carbon fiber.

Sitting in the Tub

A race car chassis is sometimes called a tub, because it resembles a bathtub. The driver sits in this tub, in a very strong compartment called the **survival cell**. This survival cell must protect the driver, so it is designed to withstand the most severe crash possible. It is made out of a "sandwich" of materials. The inside, or "filling," of the sandwich is a light but strong **honeycomb** of aluminum. The outside is carbon fiber, which shields the honeycomb. Before a new race car is allowed on a track, the survival cell must pass a series of crash tests to prove it can protect the driver in an accident.

carbon fiber (nose cone)

magnesium (wheels)

carbon fiber (body)

titanium (suspension)

carbon fiber and aluminum (survival cell)

rubber (tires)

aluminum (engine)

carbon fiber (rear wing)

SCIENCE SNAPSHOT

Although modern race cars are mostly made of carbon fiber, they do use some metals. These metals include **titanium**, **magnesium**, and **aluminum**. Like carbon fiber, the metals are strong but also light. Titanium is used for suspension parts, and magnesium is used for wheels. Aluminum is used in the chassis and to make the engine. This metal cools quickly, so it helps keep the engine from overheating.

13

I n the past, the only way a race car team could find out how well a car was running during a race was to ask the driver after the race. Today, teams receive information from cars during a race by radio. If all the information sent from each Formula One race car during a race was printed out on paper, the pile of pages would be as tall as the Empire State Building!

Collecting Data

During a race, dozens of measurements are taken from all over a race car, including engine speed, temperature, wheel speed, and even the air pressure inside the tires. This information is sent by radio to the teams at the side of the racetrack, where it appears on their computer screens. Taking measurements at a distance is called **telemetry**. It allows technicians to spot a problem even before the driver senses anything wrong with the car. The team can then tell the driver to slow down or stop before the car breaks down or has an accident.

A driver's helmet contains a radio microphone and earpieces.

SCIENCE CONCEPTS

Radio Signals

Radio signals carry information about race cars. The signals travel at the speed of light, which is 186,411 miles (300,000 km) per second! This great speed allows information from a car to reach the team at trackside in an instant. If a sensor in a car detects a problem, the information appears on the team's computer screens within one-tenth of a second!

Split-Second Timing

Race cars often cross the finish line at almost the exact same moment, so they have to be timed to within one thousandth of a second. For some races, cars have been timed to within one ten-thousandth of a second. Only electronic timing is capable of this level of accuracy.

During a race, information from race cars can be downloaded onto computers.

Onboard cameras show television viewers exactly what a race driver sees during a race.

During a race, each car transmits its own code number onto the road. **Sensors** buried under the road pick up the codes as the cars pass over them. Other systems, including high-speed cameras at the finish line, double-check the results.

Cockpit Images

Video cameras are now so small that they can be fitted into race cars to give television viewers a driver's-eye view of a race. Images from the cameras are transmitted by radio to a trackside receiver. When a camera records something interesting, the images are shown on television. If a race car is involved in an accident, its camera may be useful for investigating how the accident occurred. Cameras on cars that were near an accident can be useful, too. Their images may reveal something that people farther away were not able to see. Information from cameras can help drivers prevent accidents in the future.

SCIENCE SNAPSHOT

Devices used to identify race cars are called **transponders**. A transponder is a small electronic device, about the size of a pocket calculator. One of these devices is installed in every race car. During a race, each transponder sends out a coded radio signal that allows the racetrack's timing system to identify the car it is in.

A race car will accelerate, brake, and steer in a controlled way only if its four tires stay firmly on the ground. The wheels move up and down to stick to bumpy surfaces. If the whole car moved with the wheels, it would shake too much and be hard to control. The car is designed so only the wheels move, and the rest of the car remains steady and level.

Suspension

A race car's suspension is a system that connects the wheels to the rest of the car and allows the car to ride smoothly over bumps. This system includes springs and **shock absorbers**. Springs let wheels move upward but then push them back down. If a race car only had springs, it would bounce too much over bumps. The car also has shock absorbers, or dampers, which are usually inside the springs. The shock absorbers prevent too much bouncing. They make the wheels spring back slowly after moving upward over bumps.

Race cars are designed to stay on the track at extremely high speeds.

Ride Height

Race cars are designed to be very close to the ground. The distance between the ground and the bottom of the car's body is called its **ground clearance**. A single-seat race car's ground clearance is barely 1 inch (2.5 centimeters). As the car races along the track, most of the air that it pushes out of the way cannot go beneath it, because there is so little room. Instead, the air goes over the top of the car, where the body and wings can use the air to produce downforce. The downforce helps the car hug the track.

SCIENCE CONCEPTS

Spring Power

When you bend or squash a spring, you use energy. The spring stores this energy. When you let go, the spring releases the energy. The springs in a race car work in the same way. Every time a wheel is pushed upward by a bump in the track, the suspension spring is squashed. The spring soaks up energy and then releases it again when the wheel drops back down.

Race cars have to travel over many kinds of track surfaces.

Setting Up

Race teams adjust, or "set up," their cars differently for each race. One of the most important settings to get right is the angle, or tilt, of the wings. This angle determines how much downforce the wings will create, as well as how much drag. Another important setting is for the suspension. It can be adjusted so the car will have a harder or softer ride, to suit a particular track. If the wheels move up and down less, the ride is harder, and if the wheels move up and down more, the ride is softer. Race cars ride much harder than passenger cars, which are usually set up for comfort, not speed. Even the weather forecast for the day of a race can influence the way the team adjusts the suspension.

SCIENCE SNAPSHOT

A car rolls to one side when it takes a turn, and its nose dips when the driver brakes hard. The aerodynamics of a race car, however, work perfectly only when the car is level. A system called "active suspension" constantly adjusts itself to keep the car level all the time. Active suspension was once used in Formula One but is not allowed now.

Computers and electronics monitor every part of a race car to make sure the car always performs at its best. A computer can sense changes in the way a car is working and react to them much faster than a human driver can. Racing teams also use computers to test race cars. The computers create **simulations** of real-life race cars, race tracks, and racing conditions.

*Without **traction control**, a race car's wheels may spin too quickly.*

Computer Simulations

Some computer games feature car racing that is very realistic. Racing teams use the same technology to test race cars. A computer is programmed with a model of a car or just part of the car. The computer can then show how air flows around the car or how forces acting on it change at different speeds or in turns. Whole race tracks can be modeled, or copied, on a computer. Computer-generated cars are raced around the track to try out different ways of setting up a car for a race. These computer programs are called computer simulations, because they simulate, or imitate, the real thing.

SCIENCE CONCEPTS

Sensors

A race car has many sensors that collect information about how the car is working. A Formula One car has more than one hundred sensors. They detect changes in temperature or pressure, or the speed of various moving parts of the car, and convert them into electric currents. In this form, the information is easier to transmit through wires or by radio signals to a computer.

Programming a race car's engine control system is an important part of preparing the car for the next race.

Controlling the Engine

An electronic system controls a race car's engine. When the driver presses the car's accelerator pedal, this system senses how the pedal is moving and controls the engine so that it does what the driver wants. The system is programmed in different ways to suit each particular race track.

Traction Control

Traction is another word for the grip between a car's tires and the ground. If a driver accelerates too quickly, the powerful engine will cause the rear wheels to break their grip with the track and spin too fast. This spinning wastes engine power and slows the car. Some cars use an electronic traction control system. This system senses when wheels are about to spin. It takes control of the engine and stops the wheel-spin before it starts. Traction control is especially important in wet weather, when wheel-spin is more likely to happen. Today, traction control is not allowed in most types of car racing.

Drivers line their cars up on the starting grid for a race. They all want to leave the starting line as quickly as possible.

SCIENCE SNAPSHOT

A race car driver can get off to a bad start. The car's wheels may lose their grip and spin, or the engine may stop. An electronic system called **launch control** can make sure a driver has a perfect start every time. It feeds engine power to the wheels in exactly the right way. Launch control is not allowed, however, in most car racing, because it makes starting too easy. Formula One cars used it until 2004.

Case Study: Formula One Race Car

Formula One racing is the biggest and most popular **international** motor sport. Millions of people watch each Formula One race on television. Formula One rules give teams a lot of freedom to use advanced science and technology in their cars. The cost of designing, building, and racing these cars, however, is enormous. A successful Formula One team may have more than three hundred people working for it, and it may spend more than $365 million a year!

Aerodynamics

Every part of a Formula One car has a shape designed to reduce air resistance as much as possible and produce the most downforce. Even the shape of the driver's helmet is designed to create a smooth flow of air over the car's cockpit, to decrease drag.

Strong Forces

In a fast turn, a driver can feel a sideways force of up to five times the force of gravity. With this much force, drivers feel as if they weigh a third of a ton! Drivers have to be in excellent physical condition to deal with such powerful forces during a race.

The shape of a driver's helmet affects the air flow and drag over an open cockpit, so helmets are tested in wind tunnels to get their shape right.

A Formula One race engine is eight times more powerful than ordinary car engines, but it is less than half the weight.

"V" Power

Formula One cars have 3-liter V10 engines. Three liters is the size of the space inside each cylinder. The engines have ten cylinders arranged in the shape of a "V," with a row of five cylinders on each side. At full speed, each piston inside the engine goes up and down three hundred times a second!

Groovy Tires

In dry weather, Formula One cars used to run on completely smooth tires called slicks. These tires were eventually banned, however, so that cars could not go around turns as fast. Now, Formula One dry-weather tires must have four grooves cut in them. The grooved slicks have less rubber touching the track, so they do not grip the road as well. With less grip, drivers cannot take turns so fast. When a Formula One car is hurtling along a track at full speed, its wheels turn more than forty times per second.

This well-worn Formula One tire shows the four grooves that all Formula One dry-weather tires must have.

The modern Formula One world championship began in 1950. Today, the Formula One season usually consists of sixteen races. The races are held in Europe and other parts of the world. A Formula One car has about nine thousand parts.

Formula One car

Top speed:	224 miles (360 km) per hour
Engine:	3-liter V10
Fuel:	gasoline
Power:	900 horsepower
Minimum Weight (w/ driver):	1,322 pounds (600 kg)
Maximum Length:	13. 7 feet (4.2 m)
Maximum Width:	5.9 feet (1.8 m)
Maximum Height:	37.4 inches (95 cm)

N ASCAR race cars are called stock cars. In the early years, they used to be stock, or ordinary, cars that anyone could buy. After awhile, however, teams began to modify these cars. They installed stronger parts. Steel cages were built inside the cars to keep the roof from collapsing if the cars rolled over. More changes were made over the years. Today, a NASCAR race car looks similar to an ordinary car on the outside, but it is specially built for racing.

NASCAR drivers are outfitted with full safety gear.

Construction

A NASCAR race car starts as a pile of steel sheets and steel tubes. Workers create a frame by welding the tubes together. The front and back are made from weaker, thinner tubes than the middle of the car, where the driver sits. The weaker nose and tail are designed to collapse during a crash, soaking up some of the energy of the crash and protecting the driver. The car's frame is covered with sheets of steel, which are cut and shaped to form the body.

Front-Engine Power

The engine sits in the front of a NASCAR race car, and it drives the rear wheels. For safety, the engine is designed to be pushed downward through the bottom of the car during a head-on crash instead of backward into the driver. A thick metal plate, called a **firewall**, separates the engine and the driver's compartment. It helps stop any fires from reaching the driver.

The Plymouth Superbird, a favorite NASCAR competitor in the early 1970s, had a high rear wing.

Staying on the Ground

If a NASCAR car spins around, the same shape that makes it hug the ground when it travels forward acts like a wing when it travels tail first. If the car is going fast enough, it may actually take off and fly through the air! The cars are now fitted with flaps on the roof to solve this problem. If a car spins around, the flaps automatically pop up. They change the car's shape, so it no longer acts like a wing and does not take off.

NASCAR races are fierce, exciting competitions between closely matched cars.

A car's tail slides out on a fast turn and smoke billows from the tires. NASCAR race cars compete on oval tracks with big, sweeping turns.

Case Study: Champ Race Car

Champ cars are single-seat, open-wheel race cars. They compete in races held in the United States, Canada, and other countries. Champ cars are the fastest race cars in the world. The cars look like Formula One cars, but they are actually very different. They compete on tracks with many sharp turns, but they also race on oval tracks that have big, sweeping turns.

Champ Car Engines

Champ cars have V8 engines that are smaller than Formula One engines. The engines use turbochargers to boost power. A turbocharger is a powerful fan that blows extra air inside the engine. If it tries to blow in more air than the rules allow, a valve opens and lets the extra air out. This valve is called a pop-off valve, because when it opens, it makes a loud popping sound. Pop-off valves ensure that the engines used by all the different cars are evenly matched.

Fuel for Champ Cars

Champ car engines burn methanol instead of gasoline. Methanol is used for safety reasons. A methanol fire can easily be put out by throwing water on it, because water mixes with methanol. Water does not mix with gasoline. The gasoline will float on top of the water. When water hits burning gasoline, it can change into steam and expand so quickly that it sends the burning gasoline in all directions. One disadvantage of methanol is that it burns with an invisible flame, so fuel spilled on a car can catch fire without anyone noticing. Only someone close enough to feel the heat would notice the fire!

*A Champ car can **accelerate** from a stop to 62 miles (100 km) per hour in less than three seconds!*

*An experienced team in the **pits** can refuel a Champ car and change its wheels in a few seconds.*

Champ vs. Formula One

If a Champ car and a Formula One car raced each other on a straight level track, the Champ car would win, because it is the faster car in a straight line. On a track with many left and right turns, however, no race car can beat the best Formula One cars.

Champ cars burn fuel so quickly, they can only go about 2 miles (3.3 km) on 1 gallon (3.6 l) of methanol.

Champ car

Top speed:	236 miles (380 km) per hour
Engine:	2.65-liter turbocharged V-8
Fuel:	methanol
Power:	750 horsepower
Minimum Weight (without driver):	1,541 pounds (699kg)
Length:	15.8 to 16.3 feet (4.83 to 4.98 m)
Maximum Width:	6.6 feet (2 m)
Maximum Height:	32 inches (81cm)

Case Study: Sports Racing Car

Sports cars for the street are fast, light cars that are fun to drive, especially on twisting roads. They usually have the engine in front, turning the rear wheels. Sports cars are used in racing, too. Some sports cars are specially designed for racing. These sports racing cars are very different from ordinary sports cars.

Mid-Engine Power

A sports car designed for racing is usually a **mid-engine** car. The car has its engine in the middle, right behind the driver. The engine is the heaviest part of the car. Having it in the middle makes the car steadier and easier to handle. The engine is also close to the rear wheels, which it turns. The weight of the engine on the rear wheels helps give the tires more grip when the car is accelerating.

Sports Racing Car Bodies

The streamlined body of a sports racing car is designed to slip through the air easily and to produce great downforce, so the car can take turns faster. Some sports racing cars have a wing at the back to produce even more downforce. Ordinary sports cars usually have two seats, for a driver and a passenger. Sports racing cars never carry a passenger, but they must still have a space for a passenger seat. The driver sits to one side, instead of in the middle.

This Porsche sports car has a rear wing attached for racing.

Twenty-four Hours at the Wheel

The toughest test for sports racing cars is an **endurance** race. Endurance races last up to twenty-four hours. The most famous twenty-four-hour race is held at Le Mans in France. In twenty-four hours, the fastest cars make almost four hundred laps of the track, and they travel more than 3,107 miles (5,000 km). A team of drivers shares the driving for one car. Unlike most other race cars, the cars in this race have headlights, because they keep racing at top speed throughout the night.

Audi R8 drivers celebrate winning the twenty-four-hour Le Mans race in 2001.

Audi R8

The Audi R8 has been one of the most successful sports racing cars in recent years. The car won the Le Mans twenty-four-hour race in 2000, 2001, 2002, and 2004. It is a type of car called a Le Mans Prototype, or LMP900. This kind of car has an open cockpit and must weigh at least 1,984 pounds (900 kg). The engine can be up to 4 liters in size if turbocharged and 6 liters in size if not turbocharged. With a 3.6-liter turbocharged engine, the Audi R8 can rocket from a standstill to 62 miles (100 km) per hour in less than 3.5 seconds. An ordinary car usually takes 10 seconds or more to accelerate to the same speed.

At top speed, the Audi R8 is three times faster than an ordinary car!

Audi R8 sports racing car

Top speed:	205 miles (330 km) per hour
Engine:	3.6-liter V8, turbocharged
Fuel:	gasoline
Power:	600 horsepower
Minimum Weight:	1,984 pounds (900 kg)
Length:	15.3 feet (4.7 m)
Width:	6.6 feet (2 m)
Height:	3.5 feet (1.1 m)

The Chapparral sports car (in white) pioneered the use of wings in the late 1960s.

accelerates: increases speed.

aerodynamics: the scientific study of what happens when an object moves through the air, or when air moves around an object.

airfoil: an object, such as an airplane wing, propeller, or race car wing, that is designed to produce a certain force against a flow of air. An airplane wing produces an upward force called lift, and a race car wing produces a downward force called downforce.

aluminum: a metal used in the construction of race cars because of its light weight and ability to give off, or dissipate, heat quickly.

carbon fiber: a threadlike material that is very strong but also lightweight. When used in the construction of race cars, carbon fiber is woven into mats and then strengthened with a resin.

Champ Car World Series: a racing series for single-seat, open-wheel cars, which race on tracks in North America and other parts of the world.

chassis: a car's main frame, to which the engine, suspension, and other parts are attached.

chemists: scientists who study what things are made of and how they change.

cockpit: the place in a vehicle, such as a race car or airplane, where the vehicle is controlled.

combustion: another name for burning, a chemical reaction between fuel and air that produces heat and light.

crankshaft: a shaft at the bottom of an engine that is connected to the pistons. When the pistons move up and down, they spin the crankshaft, and this spinning motion turns the wheels.

cylinders: tubes inside an engine where combustion takes place. This combustion causes pistons in the cylinders to move up and down, spinning the crankshaft.

downforce: the downward force acting on a race car, produced by its wings and the shape of its body.

drag: also called air resistance, the force of air pushing back against a car or other object as it moves.

dragster: a kind of racing car that competes against one other car in a straight line, accelerating a short distance from a complete stop.

efficient: able to perform a job with very little waste of time or energy.

endurance: the ability to keep going, for a long period of time, despite challenging conditions.

engineering: the practice of designing and building machines, such as race cars.

firewall: a sheet of metal or other material designed to stop fire from spreading from one area of a race car to another area.

Formula One: a set of rules for the construction of single-seat, open-wheel race cars that are extremely fast. These cars compete in races held all over the world, on tracks that have many sharp turns.

friction: when objects are in contact with each other, a force that slows or stops them.

fuel: a material that is burned to produce heat or power.

fuel cell: a tough, flexible bag that holds a race car's fuel.

ground clearance: also called ride height, the distance between a car's bottom and the ground.

honeycomb: a structure that consists of many hexagons, or six-sided shapes, joined together.

horsepower: a unit of measurement for the power of an engine, originally based on how much work one horse could perform.

Indy Racing League: the organization for a race series in the United States in which single-seat, open-wheel race cars compete. The cars are similar to Champ cars and compete in races such as the Indianapolis 500.

innovations: improved products or methods.

international: involving several countries.

launch control: an electronic system designed to allow a race car driver to have a perfect start by feeding the right amount of engine power to the drive wheels.

lubricant: a substance that allows surfaces to rub together without too much heat or wear.

magnesium: a light metal often used to make parts of race cars, such as wheels.

methanol: a type of alcohol, also called methyl alcohol or wood alcohol, that is used as a fuel by some race cars.

mid-engine: having the engine in the middle, behind the driver and ahead of the rear wheels.

NASCAR: the acronym for the National Association for Stock Car Auto Racing, the organization that governs stock car racing in the United States.

physicists: scientists who study the basic building blocks of the universe and the interaction of forces between them.

pistons: cylinder-shaped pieces of metal that slide up and down inside an engine's cylinders when combustion takes place. The pistons are attached to the crankshaft, and they turn the crankshaft so it spins.

pits: the area at a race track where teams can work on their cars during a race.

polymer: a material made from long chains of small chemical units called monomers. Various kinds of plastic are made from polymers.

sensor: a device that can detect something, such as speed or heat.

shock absorbers: devices that control the force of a car's springs, so the car does not bounce too much when traveling over bumps.

simulation: a realistic imitation of an object or activity.

slick: a tire with a smooth tread that some race cars use on dry race tracks.

streamlined: having a shape that allows air to flow past smoothly.

strokes: the up and down movements of a piston inside a cylinder in a car engine.

survival cell: the compartment in a race car where the driver sits. A survival cell has to protect a driver during an accident, so it is extremely strong.

suspension: the system of parts in a car that connects the wheels to the chassis and allows the wheels to move up and down over bumps, so the car rides smoothly. This system includes springs and shock absorbers.

technology: the process of using knowledge, such as scientific discoveries, to create new products and methods.

telemetry: the process of taking measurements from a distance. In car racing, telemetry involves using sensors on cars that can send measurements by radio to team members at the side of the track.

titanium: a light metal that is very strong. It is used in the construction of aircraft and spacecraft, as well as in race cars.

traction: the grip a car's tires have on the ground.

traction control: an electronic system used on some race cars to ensure that a car's drive wheels do not lose grip and spin.

transponder: a device in a race car that transmits a coded radio signal to identify the car.

turbocharger: a fanlike device that can force more air into an engine, causing the engine to burn more fuel and produce more power. A turbocharger uses the force of exhaust gases to spin and blow air. Some race cars have turbocharged engines.

Index